DR. JOHNNY + LEZLYN PARKER

Keeping
Intimacy
Sweet +
Simple

K.I.S.S.

XO

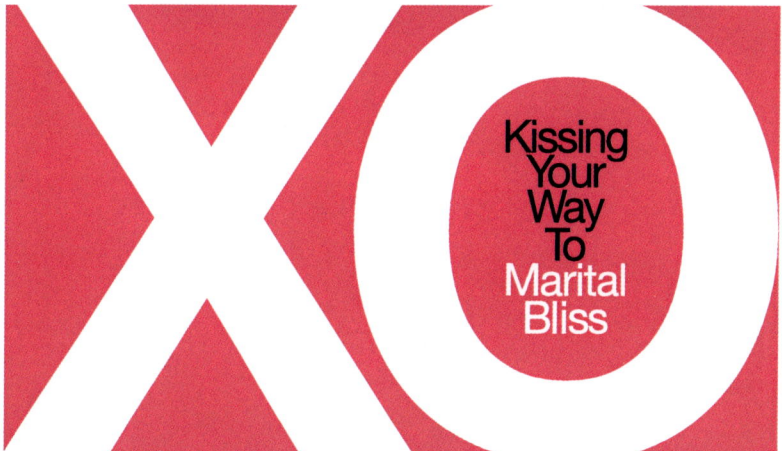

Kissing
Your
Way
To
Marital
Bliss

K.I.S.S.

Printed in the United States of America

2022 First Edition

10 9 8 7 6 5 4 3 2 1

Subject Index:
Parker, Dr. Johnny Parker & Lezlyn Parker
Title: K.I.S.S. -
Keeping Intimacy Sweet+Simple:
Kissing Your Way To Marital Bliss

1. Marriage
2. Christian Marriage
3. Love & Romance
4. Relationship Conflict Resolution
5. Love, Dating & Attraction

Paperback   ISBN 979-8-9866154-0-0

Library of Congress Card Catalog Number:
2022913346

Visit ourkiss2bliss.com for more information

THE PARKER GROUP LLC

XO

K.I.S.S.

"Dr. Johnny and Lezlyn Parker are phenomenal! They give such wise and practical wisdom! You can actually apply it to your relationships! I'm super thankful for the Parkers!"

Michelle Williams
Destiny's Child, Author of *Checking In*

"Have you ever seen a room being renovated? Just as the foreman pays close attention to the blueprints of a house being built to ensure the accuracy of the building, so must husbands and wives pay close attention to renovating their marriage room by room by the Word of God to build a successful marriage. Like an architect, Dr. Johnny Parker with metaphorical eloquence, intertwined with scriptural reference, gives us the guidelines of building a lifetime of love."

Dr. Tony Evans
Senior Pastor Oakcliff Bible Fellowship

WHAT PEOPLE ARE SAYING...

XO

"As a former NFL quarterback, I had a great opportunity to meet many people from different places and backgrounds. In life, God always puts people around you to help you along the way, and I was fortunate enough to meet one of the best there is to offer when I met Dr. Johnny Parker. He would talk to me a lot about life and my career. There are ups and downs in life, and it's hard at times to find confidence in people you can trust with the inner you. Dr. Parker is one of the few I can trust."

Jason Campbell
NFL Quarterback

K.I.S.S.

"Johnny and Lezlyn are the real deal. They are excellent communicators on the platform but even better close up: authentic, passionate, filled with grace and easy to listen to and follow. We recommend Dr. Johnny and Lezlyn Parker with 100% enthusiasm!"

Dr. Gary and Barb Rosberg
The Rosberg Group, America's Family Coaches

WHAT PEOPLE ARE SAYING...

XO

K.I.S.S.

AN HONEST ANSWER GIVEN IS LIKE A KISS ON THE LIPS.

PROVERBS 24:26

XO

DID YOU KISS YOUR SPOUSE TODAY?

It's easy to become so busy with life that we forget to kiss our spouse each day. Whether it's the responsibilities at work, family, church, or other commitments, taking a moment to reconnect with your spouse may be the key to a more fulfilling relationship. After over 30 years of marriage, my wife Lezlyn, aka "My Jamaican Sensation" regularly laughs when I lean in for a kiss and remind her, "lips matter." Although it seems simple and sounds cliché, a daily kiss can promote marital bliss. When you kiss your spouse, your brain releases your "happy hormones" such as oxytocin, dopamine, and serotonin. The simple act of kissing gives you an instant surge of positive emotions. As you lock lips, you are forming a bond which will ultimately strengthen your relationship.

LIPS MATTER

XO

BENEFITS OF KISSING YOUR SPOUSE DAILY

1 Kissing deepens your bond. Passionate kissing releases chemicals in your brain such as serotonin, dopamine and oxytocin which increases euphoria and feelings of affection.

Penn Medicine, January 8, 2018

2 Kissing reduces stress. Passionate kissing lowers cortisol levels and stress.

Western Journal of Communication, Volume 73, 2009 – Issue 20

3 Kissing adds years to your life. Men who kiss their wives before leaving for work live five years longer than husbands who don't kiss their wives.

Psychology Today, July 16, 2019

4 Kissing burns calories. Kissing is a unique way to lose weight. 5 to 26 calories per minute are being burned depending on how passionately you kiss.

The American Journal of Medicine Blog, May 28, 2013

Whether you are newlyweds or have been married for several years, it's never too late to engage in a positive habit to bring you and your spouse closer. The more you kiss, the more your body will crave the intimate emotional connection. Don't let another day go by without kissing your spouse. There's no time like the present to kiss your way to marital bliss.

LIPS MATTER

XO

DAY
1

KISS
YOUR SPOUSE
FOR A MINIMUM OF
10 SECONDS

TALK
10 MINUTE
CONVERSATION
**MY FAVORITE
MEMORY
WITH YOU...**

K.I.S.S.

XO

DAY
2

KISS

**YOUR SPOUSE
FOR A MINIMUM OF
10 SECONDS**

TALK

**10 MINUTE
CONVERSATION
I FEEL
ESPECIALLY
CLOSE TO
YOU WHEN...**

K.I.S.S.

XO

DAY
3

KISS
YOUR SPOUSE FOR A MINIMUM OF 10 SECONDS

TALK
10 MINUTE CONVERSATION

WHAT MADE YOU FALL IN LOVE WITH ME?

K.I.S.S.

XO

DAY 4

KISS

YOUR SPOUSE FOR A MINIMUM OF 10 SECONDS

TALK

10 MINUTE CONVERSATION

I FEEL CHERISHED WHEN...

K.I.S.S.

XO

DAY

5

KISS

YOUR SPOUSE
FOR A MINIMUM OF
10 SECONDS

TALK

10 MINUTE
CONVERSATION

I FEEL
ADMIRED
WHEN...

K.I.S.S.

XO

DAY

6

KISS

**YOUR SPOUSE
FOR A MINIMUM OF
10 SECONDS**

TALK

**10 MINUTE
CONVERSATION
WHAT IS
YOUR
BIGGEST
DREAM?**

K.I.S.S.

XO

DAY
7

KISS

YOUR SPOUSE
FOR A MINIMUM OF
10 SECONDS

TALK

10 MINUTE
CONVERSATION

I FEEL
LONELY
WHEN...

K.I.S.S.

XO

DAY

8

KISS

**YOUR SPOUSE
FOR A MINIMUM OF
10 SECONDS**

TALK

**10 MINUTE
CONVERSATION
WHAT DO YOU
WANT ME TO
HEAR THAT I
AM NOT
HEARING?**

K.I.S.S.

XO

DAY
9

KISS

YOUR SPOUSE
FOR A MINIMUM OF
10 SECONDS

TALK

10 MINUTE
CONVERSATION

TO MAKE OUR
RELATIONSHIP
BETTER, I AM
WILLING TO...

K.I.S.S.

XO

DAY
10

KISS

YOUR SPOUSE
FOR A MINIMUM OF
10 SECONDS

TALK

10 MINUTE
CONVERSATION

I MOST ENJOY
LOVE MAKING
WITH YOU
WHEN...

K.I.S.S.

XO

DAY
11

KISS
YOUR SPOUSE FOR A MINIMUM OF
10 SECONDS

TALK
10 MINUTE CONVERSATION
I NEED TO CONTINUE...

K.I.S.S.

XO

DAY
12

KISS
YOUR SPOUSE
FOR A MINIMUM OF
10 SECONDS

TALK
10 MINUTE
CONVERSATION

ONE THING I
NEED MORE
FROM YOU IS...

K.I.S.S.

XO

DAY
13

KISS
YOUR SPOUSE FOR A MINIMUM OF
10 SECONDS

TALK
10 MINUTE CONVERSATION
I NEED TO STOP...

K.I.S.S.

XO

DAY
14

KISS
YOUR SPOUSE
FOR A MINIMUM OF
10 SECONDS

TALK

10 MINUTE
CONVERSATION

I FEEL
ANGRY
WHEN...

K.I.S.S.

XO

DAY
15

KISS
YOUR SPOUSE
FOR A MINIMUM OF
10 SECONDS

TALK
10 MINUTE
CONVERSATION

WHAT IS
YOUR
BIGGEST
FEAR?

K.I.S.S.

XO

DAY 16

KISS

YOUR SPOUSE FOR A MINIMUM OF **10 SECONDS**

TALK

10 MINUTE CONVERSATION

K.I.S.S.

WHAT'S BECOMING CLEARER IS...

XO

DAY 17

KISS

YOUR SPOUSE FOR A MINIMUM OF 10 SECONDS

TALK

10 MINUTE CONVERSATION

WHAT CAN I DO TO MAKE YOUR LIFE EASIER TODAY?

K.I.S.S.

XO

DAY
18

KISS
YOUR SPOUSE FOR A MINIMUM OF
10 SECONDS

TALK
10 MINUTE CONVERSATION

IT'S GETTING HARDER FOR ME TO...

K.I.S.S.

XO

KISS
YOUR SPOUSE
FOR A MINIMUM OF
10 SECONDS

TALK
10 MINUTE
CONVERSATION

WHAT'S THE BEST DECISION YOU EVER MADE OTHER THAN MARRYING ME?

K.I.S.S.

XO

DAY
20

KISS
**YOUR SPOUSE
FOR A MINIMUM OF
10 SECONDS**

TALK
**10 MINUTE
CONVERSATION**

**IF WE TRY I
BELIEVE WE
CAN....**

K.I.S.S.

XO

DAY
21

KISS

YOUR SPOUSE
FOR A MINIMUM OF
10 SECONDS

TALK

10 MINUTE
CONVERSATION

IN WHAT
SITUATIONS
DO YOU FEEL
LOVED BY ME?

K.I.S.S.

XO

DAY 22

KISS

YOUR SPOUSE FOR A MINIMUM OF 10 SECONDS

TALK

10 MINUTE CONVERSATION

WHAT ONE THING CAN I DO TO HELP YOU FEEL EMOTIONALLY SAFE?

K.I.S.S.

XO

KISS

YOUR SPOUSE
FOR A MINIMUM OF
10 SECONDS

TALK

10 MINUTE
CONVERSATION

I NEED
TO
START...

K.I.S.S.

XO

DAY
24

KISS

YOUR SPOUSE
FOR A MINIMUM OF
10 SECONDS

TALK

10 MINUTE
CONVERSATION

**WHAT DO
I MEAN
TO YOU?**

K.I.S.S.

XO

DAY
25

KISS
YOUR SPOUSE
FOR A MINIMUM OF
10 SECONDS

TALK
10 MINUTE
CONVERSATION

WHEN DO
YOU FEEL
HEARD
BY ME?

K.I.S.S.

XO

DAY

26

KISS

YOUR SPOUSE
FOR A MINIMUM OF
10 SECONDS

TALK

10 MINUTE
CONVERSATION

I FEEL
APPRECIATED
BY YOU WHEN...

K.I.S.S.

XO

DAY
27

KISS
YOUR SPOUSE
FOR A MINIMUM OF
10 SECONDS

TALK

10 MINUTE
CONVERSATION
PLEASE
HELP
ME TO...

K.I.S.S.

XO

DAY

28

KISS

YOUR SPOUSE FOR A MINIMUM OF 10 SECONDS

TALK

10 MINUTE CONVERSATION

WHEN WE TRAVEL I FEEL...

K.I.S.S.

XO

DAY
29

KISS
YOUR SPOUSE FOR A MINIMUM OF 10 SECONDS

TALK
10 MINUTE CONVERSATION

WHERE DO YOU SEE US IN THE NEXT THREE YEARS?

K.I.S.S.

XO

DAY

30

KISS

YOUR SPOUSE FOR A MINIMUM OF

10 SECONDS

TALK

10 MINUTE CONVERSATION

K.I.S.S.

WHAT'S SOMETHING NEW ABOUT ME THAT YOU LIKE?

XO

DAY
31

KISS
YOUR SPOUSE
FOR A MINIMUM OF
10 SECONDS

TALK
10 MINUTE
CONVERSATION

**WHAT DO YOU
BELIEVE ARE
OUR TOP THREE
STRENGTHS AS
A COUPLE?**

K.I.S.S.

XO

KISS

**YOUR SPOUSE
FOR A MINIMUM OF
10 SECONDS**

TALK

**10 MINUTE
CONVERSATION**

K.I.S.S.

WHAT'S THE BEST VACATION WE HAVE TAKEN AS A COUPLE?

XO

KISS

YOUR SPOUSE FOR A MINIMUM OF 10 SECONDS

TALK

10 MINUTE CONVERSATION

WHAT BOOK HAS IMPACTED YOU THE MOST? WHY?

K.I.S.S.

XO

KISS

**YOUR SPOUSE
FOR A MINIMUM OF
10 SECONDS**

TALK

**10 MINUTE
CONVERSATION**

K.I.S.S.

**WHAT
MAKES
OUR
RELATIONSHIP
SPECIAL?**

XO

KISS

YOUR SPOUSE
FOR A MINIMUM OF
10 SECONDS

TALK

10 MINUTE
CONVERSATION

WHAT
IS GOD
TEACHING
YOU?

K.I.S.S.

XO

DAY
36
KISS
YOUR SPOUSE
FOR A MINIMUM OF
10 SECONDS

TALK
10 MINUTE
CONVERSATION
WHEN WE
PRAY
TOGETHER
I FEEL...

K.I.S.S.

XO

DAY
37

KISS

YOUR SPOUSE
FOR A MINIMUM OF
10 SECONDS

TALK

10 MINUTE
CONVERSATION

WHEN WE
READ THE
BIBLE
TOGETHER
I FEEL...

K.I.S.S.

XO

38

KISS
YOUR SPOUSE
FOR A MINIMUM OF
10 SECONDS

TALK
10 MINUTE
CONVERSATION

WHEN DO
YOU FEEL
CLOSEST
TO GOD?

K.I.S.S.

XO

DAY
39

KISS

YOUR SPOUSE
FOR A MINIMUM OF
10 SECONDS

TALK

10 MINUTE
CONVERSATION

**WHAT'S ONE
THING YOU
ALWAYS
WANTED TO
LEARN
ABOUT ME?**

K.I.S.S.

XO

DAY
40

KISS
YOUR SPOUSE FOR A MINIMUM OF
10 SECONDS

TALK
10 MINUTE CONVERSATION

WE ARE AT OUR BEST WHEN WE...

K.I.S.S.

XO

DAY
41

KISS
**YOUR SPOUSE
FOR A MINIMUM OF
10 SECONDS**

TALK

10 MINUTE
CONVERSATION

**WHILE GROWING
UP, WHAT WERE
YOUR EARLIEST
MEMORIES
ABOUT
MONEY?**

K.I.S.S.

XO

KISS

YOUR SPOUSE FOR A MINIMUM OF
10 SECONDS

TALK

10 MINUTE CONVERSATION

I FEEL ESPECIALLY CLOSE TO YOU WHEN...

K.I.S.S.

XO

KISS

**YOUR SPOUSE
FOR A MINIMUM OF
10 SECONDS**

TALK

**10 MINUTE
CONVERSATION**

K.I.S.S.

**WHAT NEW
THINGS
SHOULD
WE DO
TOGETHER?**

XO

DAY
44

KISS
YOUR SPOUSE
FOR A MINIMUM OF
10 SECONDS

TALK
10 MINUTE
CONVERSATION

WHAT'S
YOUR
FAVORITE
PLACE TO
BE WITH
ME?

K.I.S.S.

XO

DAY 45

KISS
YOUR SPOUSE FOR A MINIMUM OF 10 SECONDS

TALK
10 MINUTE CONVERSATION

WHAT'S ONE FINANCIAL GOAL YOU WOULD LIKE FOR US TO ACHIEVE?

K.I.S.S.

XO

DAY
46
KISS
YOUR SPOUSE
FOR A MINIMUM OF
10 SECONDS

TALK
10 MINUTE
CONVERSATION
WHAT'S ONE
THING THAT
MAKES OUR
RELATIONSHIP
STRONG?

K.I.S.S.

XO

DAY
47

KISS
YOUR SPOUSE
FOR A MINIMUM OF
10 SECONDS

TALK
10 MINUTE
CONVERSATION

K.I.S.S.

WHAT
THREE
THINGS
ARE YOU
GRATEFUL
FOR?

XO

DAY
48

KISS

**YOUR SPOUSE
FOR A MINIMUM OF
10 SECONDS**

TALK

**10 MINUTE
CONVERSATION**

WHAT GAVE
YOU LIFE
TODAY?

K.I.S.S.

XO

DAY
49

KISS
YOUR SPOUSE FOR A MINIMUM OF
10 SECONDS

TALK
10 MINUTE CONVERSATION

HOW CAN I BECOME EASIER TO LIVE WITH?

K.I.S.S.

XO

DAY
50

KISS

YOUR SPOUSE
FOR A MINIMUM OF
10 SECONDS

TALK

10 MINUTE
CONVERSATION

WHAT THREE
ACCOMPLISHMENTS
ARE YOU MOST
PROUD OF?

K.I.S.S.

XO

DAY
51

KISS
YOUR SPOUSE
FOR A MINIMUM OF
10 SECONDS

TALK
10 MINUTE
CONVERSATION

WHAT THREE
EXPERIENCES
ARE YOU
LOOKING
FORWARD TO
IN THE NEXT
10 DAYS?

K.I.S.S.

xo

DAY
52

KISS

YOUR SPOUSE
FOR A MINIMUM OF
10 SECONDS

TALK

10 MINUTE
CONVERSATION

WHAT HAVE
YOU ENJOYED
MOST ABOUT
OUR KISS 2
BLISS
EXPERIENCE?

XO

K.I.S.S.

Dr. Johnny and Lezlyn Parker are relationship architects who help couples build marriages that flourish. They are the founders of The Parker Group, LLC which provides leadership/relationship development and coaching.

They have spoken nationally for FamilyLife's "Weekend To Remember" marriage conferences for over 10 years and provide services to pro athletes and high-performing leaders.

OurKiss2Bliss.com

XO

Whether you are newlyweds or have been married for several years, it's never too late to engage in a positive habit to bring you and your spouse closer. The Parkers have created a simple marital tool that will strengthen your relationship for years. Regular kissing has several benefits, including: deepening your bond and adding years to your life. Make every day count by kissing your way to marital bliss.

$18.99
ISBN 979-8-9866154-0-0
51899>

9 798986 615400

THE
PARKER
GROUP

58011122R00035

Made in the USA
Middletown, DE
26 July 2024

58011122R00035